Growing Up in
Religious Communities

THE CHANGING FACE OF MODERN FAMILIES

Adoptive Parents

Blended Families

Celebrity Families

Families Living with Mental
& Physical Challenges

First-Generation Immigrant Families

Foster Families

Gay and Lesbian Parents

Grandparents Raising Kids

Growing Up in Religious Communities

Kids Growing Up Without a Home

Multiracial Families

Single Parents

Teen Parents

What Is a Family?

Growing Up in
Religious Communities

Sheila Stewart

Mason Crest Publishers, Inc.

MASON CREST PUBLISHERS INC.
370 Reed Road
Broomall, Pennsylvania 19008
(866)MCP-BOOK (toll free)
www.masoncrest.com

First Printing

9 8 7 6 5 4 3 2 1

ISBN 978-1-4222-1500-5
ISBN 978-1-4222-1490-9 (series)
Library of Congress Cataloging-in-Publication Data
Stewart, Sheila.

Produced by Harding House Publishing Service, Inc. www.hardinghousepages.com
Interior Design by MK Bassett-Harvey.
Cover design by Asya Blue www.asyablue.com.
Printed in The United States of America.

Although the families whose stories are told in this book are made up of real people, in some cases their names have been changed to protect their privacy.

Photo Credits

Creative Commons Attribution ShareAlike: diluvi 35, laverrue 23, masukomi 53, myshi 9; Dreamstime: Robertplotz 10, Schulz, Jay M. 33, Young, Lisa F. 12; GNU Free Documentation License: Lokal_Profil 50; United States Department of Defense: Houlihan, Robert 26

Contents

Introduction   6
1. Religion and Families   8
2. A Muslim in America   16
3. An Amish Artist   32
4. Growing Up in a Conservative Christian Group   48
Find Out More   60
Bibliography   62
Index   63
About the Author and the Consultant   64

Introduction

The Gallup Poll has become synonymous with accurate statistics on what people really think, how they live, and what they do. Founded in 1935 by statistician Dr. George Gallup, the Gallup Organization continues to provide the world with unbiased research on who we really are.

From recent Gallup Polls, we can learn a great deal about the modern family. For example, a June 2007 Gallup Poll reported that Americans, on average, believe the ideal number of children for a family to have these days is 2.5. This includes 56 percent of Americans who think it is best to have a small family of one, two, or no children, and 34 percent who think it is ideal to have a larger family of three or more children; nine percent have no opinion. Another recent Gallup Poll found that when Americans were asked, "Do you think homosexual couples should or should not have the legal right to adopt a child," 49 percent of Americans said they should, and 48 percent said they shouldn't; 43 percent supported the legalization of gay marriage, while 57 percent did not. Yet another poll found that 34 percent of Americans feel a conflict between the demands of their professional life and their family life; 39 percent still believe that one parent should ideally stay home with the children while the other works.

Keep in mind that Gallup Polls do not tell us what is right or wrong. They don't report on what people should think—only on what they do think. And what is clear from Gallup Polls is that while the shape of families is changing in our modern world, the concept of family is still vital to our sense of who we are and how we interact with others. An indication of this is the 2008 Gallup poll that found that three out of four Americans reported that family values are important, while one in three said they are "extremely" important.

And how do Americans define "family values"? According to the same poll, here's what Americans say is their definition of a family: a strong unit where faith and morals, education and integrity play important roles within the structure of a committed relationship.

The books in the series demonstrate that strong family units come in all shapes and sizes. Those differences, however, do not change the faith, integrity, and commitment of the families who tell their stories within these books.

1 Religion and Families

What does the phrase "religious community" mean to you? Do you immediately think of a closed off group, having no contact with the rest of the world? Do you think of a certain religion or group? Do you think about your own faith tradition?

Many different types of religious communities exist in North America and around the world. The distinguishing feature of these communities is that they are somehow separate from the world around them—in how they dress or what they may or may not eat or what they are *prohibited* from doing. Some of these communities truly are closed off from the rest of the world, having little contact with those outside the community. Some groups keep their religious practices secret from those

8

who are not a member of the community. Other communities mingle with the people around them, despite the ways they have separated themselves.

Religion is a part of many people's lives, whether or not they consider themselves part of a religious community. What people believe about a *deity*, or about how the universe and people came to be created, shapes their *morals* and their actions. For those growing up in a

This father and his daughters are members of the Satmar community in Williamsburg, Brooklyn, NY. Satmar is a branch of Hasidic Judaism started by Hungarian and Romanian Holocaust survivors.

religious community, though, these beliefs and practices are a large part of everyday life.

There are both good and bad things about growing up in a family that is a part of a religious community, just like there are good and bad things about growing up in any family. For example, many who grew up with a strict religious tradition have found later in life that their upbringing gives them a sense of stability, even if they are no longer a part of that tradition.

Studies have shown that children in religious families are often more well-adjusted and better behaved than children in families where religion does not play a large role. Another study points out that this does not necessarily mean they are

Researchers from the University of British Columbia have done a study that indicates a personal belief system (spirituality) is more important to an adolescent's happiness than organized religious practices.

happier; this study found that spirituality—a person's individual belief system—is more of a key to happiness than religious practices alone. So just growing up in a religious family isn't enough to make you happy (or unhappy); other circumstances affect you, of course, and what you think and believe about your religion make a big difference.

Psychologist Erika Chopich, in her article "Do Children Need Religion?" writes about the benefits of being raised in a religious tradition. She believes that children need to know that there is something greater than themselves, and that religion teaches them self-discipline, *empathy*, and humility as well. Dr. Chopin believes that her early religious training gave her perspective and that those who are raised without religion can grow up to be *egotistical* adults; they have come to believe that they are the center of the world, the most important thing in their own universe. "I am not the center," writes Dr. Chopin, "but rather, a necessary part of a great whole."

Those who want to raise their children without the influence of religion often have bad memories of how they were forced to attend church as a young person or of how many members of their religion seemed to be *hypocrites*, living lives that did not match up with the things they said they believed. Some point to the evil things that have been done throughout history in the name of religion, and they want to raise their children

There are more than 400 recognized Christian religious organizations/ church groups in the United States alone. This number does not include the many non-Christian religious groups that exist as well.

11

GROWING UP IN
RELIGIOUS COMMUNITIES

apart from such hatred. Religious leaders have too often not lived up to the standards their tradition sets for them, sometimes to the point of misusing their position and the respect people give them. The fact that only a small percentage of religious leaders are involved in such things does not really matter, since many people have connected scandal with religion in their minds.

Small, close-knit religious communities have the advantage of giving families a lot of support. They share the joys and high points of each others' lives and they are there to help out when anyone is sick or going through financial trouble or dealing with the death of another

family member. When these communities work as they are meant to, no one has to feel alone when facing difficult times. The disadvantage of such communities is that when things go wrong—such as abuse by a leader, for example—people within the situation often feel they have nowhere to turn.

The people whose stories are told in this book are aware of the positives and negatives of their upbringing in a religious community. Even when they are no longer a part of that community, they understand how it has shaped their lives.

HEADLINES

(Fagan, Patrick F. "Why Religion Matters Even More: The Impact of Religious Practice on Social Stability." *Backgrounder*. 18 Dec. 2006. http://www.heritage.org/research/religion/bg1992.cfm)

Over the past decade, considerable research has emerged that demonstrates the benefits of religious practice within society. Religious practice promotes the well-being of individuals, families, and the community.

Of particular note are the studies that indicate the benefits of religion to the poor. Regular attendance at religious services is linked to healthy, stable family life, strong marriages, and well-behaved children. The practice of religion also leads to a reduction in

According to a recent Gallup poll, compared with individuals who seldom or never attended religious services, individuals who attended services at least once a week were nearly twice as likely to report being very happy with their lives and a third more likely to say they were *optimistic* about the future.

the incidence of domestic abuse, crime, substance abuse, and addiction. In addition, religious practice leads to an increase in physical and mental health, longevity, and education attainment. Moreover, these effects are intergenerational, as grandparents and parents pass on the benefits to the next generations.

America's Founding Fathers understood the vital role that religion plays in a free society. Far from shielding the American people from religious influence, the Founders promoted the freedom of religion and praised the benefits that it brings to society. George Washington articulated this in his farewell address to the nation:

Of all the *dispositions* and habits which lead to political prosperity, Religion and Morality are *indispensable* supports. In vain would that man claim the tribute of Patriotism who should labor to subvert these great Pillars of human happiness—these firmest props of the duties of Men and citizens. The mere Politician, equally with the *pious* man, ought to respect and to cherish them. A volume could not trace all their connections with private and public felicity. Let it simply be asked, Where is the security for property, for reputation, for life, if the sense of religious obligation desert the oaths, which are the instruments of investigation in Courts of Justice? And let us with caution indulge the *sup-*

position that morality can be maintained without religion. Whatever may be *conceded* to the influence of refined education on minds of *peculiar* structure, reason and experience both forbid us to expect that National morality can prevail in exclusion of religious principle.

Given the extent to which religious practice promotes civil society, understanding religion's contribution to America's *constitutional* order is *fundamental* to the nation's continued prosperity. The practice of religion is a powerful *antidote* to many of our nation's pressing social problems, many of which have reached historically high proportions. Yet, despite the societal benefits of religion, the expression of faith in the public square has faced many challenges. Therefore, legislators should seek constitutionally appropriate ways to explore the impact of religious practice on society and, where appropriate, recognize its role and importance.

What Do You Think?

Describe the viewpoint of this author in your own words. Do you agree or disagree? How important do you feel religion is to the community where you live?

Chapter 2: A Muslim in America

As soon as Eboo Patel could talk, his mother began teaching him the special prayers that Ismaili Muslims recited every morning and evening. When he was just a baby, his family moved from India to the United States, where his father earned an MBA at Notre Dame and then moved the family to Chicago where he had a marketing job.

In his early childhood, his life was filled with the rituals of his religion: "Morning and evening, my family would gather for prayer, hands cupped to receive blessings, forehead and nose touching the ground in *sijda*, prayer beads sliding through our fingers as we chanted, 'Ya Allah, Ya Allah' (Oh God, Oh God)." He learned the Ismaili devotional songs from his grandmother and led his local congregation in prayers when he was still very young.

As Eboo grew up, however, he found himself rebelling against the differences between himself and his white American classmates. He was bullied in school, taunted for being Indian and for being Muslim. His parents didn't understand: "My mother was convinced that if I would only raise my math grade, the other kids would respect me. 'Say your *tasbih*,' she would add, referring to the Muslim prayer beads. It made me feel worse to tell her what happened in school, so I stopped."

As his parents became absorbed in their jobs and the details of their daily lives, many of the rituals of their religion fell away, consumed by the busyness of everyday life. This did not mean Islam no longer played a role in Eboo's life. For one thing, he still did not eat pork. On a class camping trip, while the others ate sausage or pepperoni pizza, Eboo ate the slice of cheese pizza his mother had insisted the school provide for him. At birthday parties, she would call ahead to find out what the food would be. "If hot dogs were the order of the day," Eboo writes, "she would hand me a plastic bag with two beef frank-

Terms to Understand

bigotry: intolerance and indifference toward beliefs and opinions that are different than one's own.

radical: a person who hold extreme views and often believes in direct and unconventional action to achieve social reform.

oppression: using authority and power in cruel, burdensome, and unjust ways.

imperialism: the policy of extending a country's influence or authority over foreign countries or colonies.

activist: passionate supporter or opponent of a cause.

pluralism: the accepted presence of a variety of ethnic, religious, or cultural groups, and the belief that such a variety is a good and beneficial thing.

empowering: giving power or authority to.

ethnicities: relating to ethnic groups and having the cultural traits and backgrounds connected with these groups.

Islam is not a new religion, but the same truth that God revealed through all His prophets to every people. For a fifth of the world's population, Islam is both a religion and a complete way of life. Muslims follow a religion of peace, mercy, and forgiveness, and the majority have nothing to do with the extremely grave events which have come to be associated with their faith. . . .

Muhammad was born in Makkah in the year 570, at a time when Christianity was not yet fully established in Europe. Since his father died before his birth, and his mother shortly afterwards, he was raised by his uncle from the respected tribe of Quraysh. As he grew up, he became known for his truthfulness, *generosity* and sincerity, so that he was sought after for his ability to *arbitrate* in disputes. The historians describe him as calm and *meditative*.

Muhammad was of a deeply religious nature, and had long detested the *decadence* of his society. It became his habit to meditate from time to time in the Cave of Hira near the summit of Jabal al-Nur, the "Mountain of Light" near Makkah.

At the age of 40, while engaged in a meditative retreat, Muhammad received his first *revelation* from God through the Angel Gabriel. This revelation, which continued for twenty-three years, is known as the Quran.

As soon as he began to recite the words he heard from Gabriel, and to preach the truth which God had revealed to him, he and his small group of followers suffered bitter *persecution*, which grew so fierce that in the year 622 God gave them the command to emigrate. This event, the Hijra, "migration," in which they left Makkah for the city of Madinah some 260 miles to the north, marks the beginning of the Muslim calendar.

After several years, the Prophet and his followers were able to return to Makkah, where they forgave their enemies and established Islam definitively. Before the Prophet died at the age of 63, the greater part of Arabia was Muslim, and within a century of his death Islam had spread to Spain in the West and as far East as China. . . .

The Quran, the last revealed Word of God, is the *prime* source of every Muslim's faith and practice. It deals with all the subjects which concern us as human beings: wisdom, doctrine, worship, and law, but its basic theme is the relationship between God and His creatures. At the same time it provides guidelines for a just society, proper human conduct and an *equitable* economic system. . . .

[The Five Pillars of Islam] are the framework of the Muslim life: faith, prayer, concern for the needy, *self-purification*, and the *pilgrimage* to Makkah for those who are able.

(from *Understanding Islam and the Muslims*, prepared by The Islamic Affairs Department, The Embassy of Saudi Arabia, Washington DC. on www.islamicity.com)

furters and tell me to remind whoever was cooking to use a separate pan."

Eboo was embarrassed by the special treatment. He wanted to fit in, to be like everyone else as much as he could. He didn't understand what the big deal was. When he asked, his mother got angry. "Because we are Muslims," she yelled. "We do not eat pork."

Although he experienced bullying in school, Eboo found it difficult to support a Jewish friend when a group of other kids started shouting anti-Semitic insults in the halls and writing them on desks. This is what he is most ashamed of today. "I did not confront them. I did not comfort my Jewish friend. Instead I averted my eyes from their bigotry, and I avoided my friend because I couldn't stand to face him," he writes. Years later, his friend talked with him about the experience, telling Eboo how afraid and abandoned he had felt during that time.

In college, Eboo suddenly came face to face with his cultural identity. Everything he had previously rejected, he suddenly embraced with fervor. He became a *radical*, talking of white *oppression* and American *imperialism*. His father was

Terms to Understand

incomprehensible: impossible to understand.
norms: general levels, averages, or standards.
mandatory: required, ordered.
ethnographic: related to the branch of anthropology that scientifically describes specific human cultures.
tenets: doctrines, opinions, and principles held by members of a group.
assimilate: conform, adapt to the customs, styles, and behaviors of a group or culture.
sequestered: set apart, isolated.
conservative: traditional; wishing to preserve the traditional customs, practices, and beliefs and opposing change.
stereotype: an oversimplified standard image or idea held in common by a large number of people.

exasperated with him when he came home, bothered by Eboo's political extremes. Meanwhile, Eboo found he understood the anger—the rage—that led to acts of terrorist violence.

But Eboo was not violent himself, and perhaps the habit of volunteering that his parents had encouraged in him growing up was what led him away from this vio-

The United States Muslim population is growing—since 1990 the number of people identifying themselves as Muslim rose from 0.3% to 0.6%. In contrast, the total number of people identifying themselves as Christian fell 10.2% from 1990 to 2008.

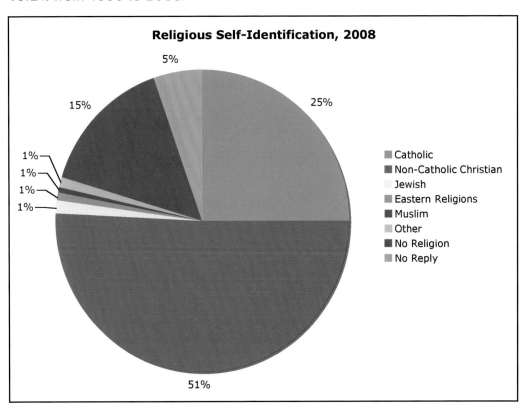

Religious Self-Identification, 2008

5%
15%
25%
1%
1%
1%
1%
51%

- Catholic
- Non-Catholic Christian
- Jewish
- Eastern Religions
- Muslim
- Other
- No Religion
- No Reply

The two main types of Muslims are Sunnis and Shiites, but there are many smaller divisions. Ninety percent of Muslims are Sunnis.

lence. He had been a part of the YMCA Leaders Club as a young person, and when he had wanted to stop volunteering there, his parents had refused. They told him that volunteering and helping others was part of what it meant to be an Ismaili Muslim. "Your father's faith is very strong," his mother told him. "For him, faith is about service, not rituals. His family in India has been involved in service at every level imaginable. One day you will hear the stories. They will make you proud." So Eboo continued to volunteer. He writes,

And so I spent my Saturday mornings teaching swimming lessons to handicapped people at the YMCA. I spent every afternoon at the Y during the weeks before Halloween and Easter helping to set up the haunted house and the Easter egg hunt. I learned something about the lives of people unlike me. I learned to cheer for someone other than myself.

At college, Eboo continued to volunteer, helping out at a nursing home, a women's shelter, and the Salvation Army. He felt he needed the connection with other people. His college friends didn't understand. They thought social service agencies were part of a larger, corrupt system in the United States, and that Eboo was betraying his politics to spend time there. Even those friends who did volunteer, seemed to do so just to make

This young woman in New York City stands out because of her red hijab. Muslim teenagers in America may not like this feeling of standing out or being different from their peers because of the questions and possible prejudices that it will cause.

themselves feel good. Nobody wanted to talk to Eboo about the larger problems and what solutions could be found for them.

Then, Eboo came across the Catholic Worker movement, which had been founded in 1933 to promote jus-

Muslims are required to avoid pork and pork products and not to drink alcohol. They also must avoid eating or drinking blood or food with blood in it, as well as animals that have been killed in certain ways.

tice and charity for those who were poor or hurting. "I was tired of raging," Eboo writes. "It left me feeling empty, and what did it achieve anyway? I wanted to improve people's lives because I loved humanity, not because I hated the system. Sometimes, I thought, my *activist* friends hated the system more than they loved humanity." It didn't matter to the other Catholic Workers that Eboo was Muslim, and they did not try to convert him.

His work with the YMCA and with the Catholic Workers, and his experience with his diverse group of friends throughout his life, had helped Eboo learn to be accepting and understanding of other religions. In 1998, he and his friend Kevin, who was Jewish, decided to form a group designed to encourage interfaith understanding and discussions between young people. They became founding members of the Interfaith Youth Core (IFYC). The mission of the Core is to build "mutual respect and *pluralism* among young people from different religious traditions by *empowering* them to work together to serve others."

Today, Eboo's driving mission is religious pluralism and how to help people of different religious backgrounds work together for common causes. His wife works with him, and he says that she "embodies in human form so many of the central values of the Muslim tradition—compassion, mercy, patience, and constancy."

What Do You Think?

What role did his family play in Eboo's religious beliefs? How did his parents' shape who he became? What role do you think your parents play in what you believe?

HEADLINES

(From "American Muslim Teenagers: Torn Between Religion and Culture" by Farad Faruqui, *Watan: Arab American Newspaper*, 21 December 2008, http://www.watan.com/en/the-community/165-american-muslim-teenagers-torn-between-religion-and-culture.html)

The United States is home to Muslims from all walks of life and *ethnicities*. Some are immigrants and others are born and reared Americans; yet, that does not diminish the difficulties Muslim youth sometimes face on account of their religious identity.

When Shyma Al-Shoeb migrated to the United States from Saudi Arabia in 1997, she was tested into the 10th grade, but chose to step down to 8th grade so that she could sit with her younger brother in school.

Her choice may seem unreasonable, even *incomprehensible*, but one has to accept that it is hard for anyone to get adjusted to a new culture, let alone the idea of other students mocking you for your culture, garb and practice.

GROWING UP IN RELIGIOUS COMMUNITIES

The September 11, 2001, attacks on the World Trade Center in New York City and the Pentagon in Washington, D.C. (shown here), led to an increase in prejudice against Muslim Americans.

"I preferred isolation and loneliness," said Al-Shoeb. "I did not like to be asked questions: Why are you not eating, if it is not Ramadan? Why do you cover up? Do you have a boyfriend? How do you feel about going out with me?"

Muslim teenagers—both American born and first generation immigrants—are torn between the *norms* and values taught at home and the youth culture of public high schools in the U.S.

Al-Shoeb was a young girl with strong feelings of being out of place in a school environment before 9/11. But when compared with the hostility Muslim students endured after 9/11, the questions that Al-Shoeb once faced, before the terrorist attacks, seem bland and curious.

Noura Badawi, a teacher at Schenectady High School in upstate New York, where almost five percent of the student population is from a Muslim background, has observed widespread discrimination against Muslim students.

"Some of my students reported being called names, being threatened, being left out, and that they feel lonely and sometimes on the defense as a result," said Badawi. "It became cool to make a spectacle of, ridicule, insult and pick a fight with Muslim kids, innocent or not, because this was so widely accepted in the media," she added.

Dr Louis Abdellatif Cristillo, a professor at Teachers College, Columbia University, studied experiences of Muslim boys and girls in New York City public high schools in a recently completed three-year research initiative.

Funded by the Ford Foundation, the project collected data on how the post-9/11 school climate has impacted the lives and attitudes of youth, especially in

regard to their personal identification as Muslims and Americans.

Educators have studied gang violence, poverty, achievement problems and language barriers between Christian and Jewish youth. But no one has yet added to the understanding of Muslim youth in the U.S. and their distinct needs as the fastest growing religious minority in public schools, said Cristillo.

Muslim parents in 2006, for example, had to make the bitter choice between sending their children to school for the *mandatory* statewide Regents exam—an exam that could affect their future—or being marked absent in order to celebrate Eid-ul-Adha with their families.

What interested him most, Cristillo said, is the impact of the post-9/11 school climate on Muslim students' feelings of being accepted into or excluded from the American mainstream.

Cristillo, along with his research assistant Muntasir Sattar, interviewed 633 high school students as part of his research, of an estimated 100,000 Muslim students in New York City Public Schools.

The research also included focus groups of students and key adult stakeholders such as teachers, guidance counselors and parents, in addition to *ethno-*

graphic interviews inside a high school, conducted by Dr Ameena Ghaffar-Kucher.

"Psychologically, the youth is stressed out to confirm and perform," said Cristillo.

Like other religions, Islam prescribes certain dos and don'ts in relation to dress, social norms, culture and dietary restrictions. At times, these *tenets* and teachings can be difficult to adhere to—especially in a student community that is ignorant or misinformed of your belief system which does not understand your religious sentiments, remarked Cristillo.

As an educator, trained in Teachers College at Columbia University, Noura Badawi pinpointed the confusion that has clouded many young and fertile minds. "Muslim teenagers are very conflicted; they have a need to *assimilate*, but they also have a strong desire to please their parents and their community," she said.

"Sometimes the pressure is so great that the teenagers go the complete opposite direction or break free by moving away as soon as an opportunity comes up."

For example, a headscarf is considered to be a mandatory part of the traditional Islamic dress code for women, but it is often associated by Western people with female oppression.

"The constant cracks at Muslims in general are enough to make the girls feel different, misunderstood, hurt and secluded" said Badawi.

"This is especially true for those girls who wear hijab. Some of them removed it out of insecurity and fear of being singled out, targeted, and being the butt of a joke," she added.

"At the beginning, I didn't cover up, but I dressed up modestly, until I saw another girl pass by in the cafeteria, wearing a hijab, which gave me the will and the confidence to start wearing it again and embrace my identity as an Arab-Muslim," said Al-Shoeb, the student who had emigrated from Saudi Arabia.

High school is particularly difficult for teenage Muslim girls, said Cristillo, because they often are much more *sequestered* than boys, especially those who come from *conservative* families.

"It is often young girls, more than boys, who must consciously negotiate their identity in public," said Cristillo.

Some boys who shave and groom themselves like other kids in the school can hide their ethnic background, Cristillo said, but the *stereotype* that young Muslim men pose a threat continues to be a problem for many high schoolers.

"A man with a beard on a subway is usually feared by other passengers because he resembles the terrorists they see on television," said Sattar, Cristillo's research assistant.

The way Muslim boys are profiled in the post September 11 era is counterproductive, said Sattar, and boys—especially those who grow beards for religious reasons—are labeled by other students as politically charged individuals and dangerous.

"The US government's anti-terrorism policies have sowed the fear of homegrown Islamic radicalism in the American consciousness," said Cristillo.

What Do You Think?

How does prejudice play a role in Muslim families? This article indicates that the prejudice against Muslims has become worse since 9/11. Why do you think this is true? Have you experienced this in your community?

3 An Amish Artist

Every week, Susie tries to paint at least ten or fifteen hours. She works in watercolors at her kitchen table. At one time, she worried that her art conflicted with her Amish heritage and lifestyle. This has been an ongoing concern in her life.

Susie has always loved to draw, to color, to paint. It was her favorite part of school, and her teacher nurtured her gift. When she left school, at the end of eighth grade, she continued to draw and paint, but only occasionally. "It seemed," her friend Louise Stoltzfus writes, "that her sensibilities as an Amish young person provided little room for the idea that she might be an artist. Painting became a secondary interest, but the passion never left."

Susie and John have six children now, the youngest a toddler and the oldest a teenager. Between the time Susie and John married and the time their first child was born, she barely painted at all. Life was spent working on John's father's farm, milking cows and working

Terms to Understand

sustain: support, hold up.
mystique: a quality of mystery surrounding something, giving it added value or interest.
ultraconservative: extremely conservative, that is, unwilling to change tradition or accept new ideas.
impasse: a position from which there is no escape; stalemate.

in the fields. Sometimes Susie taught at the little Amish school just down the road as well. There was almost no time left over for art. Still, Susie later wondered if she should have been finding time to paint during that period, before the babies came. On the other hand, Louise writes, Susie believes that "perhaps she needed the children to give her the sense of personal fulfillment required to *sustain* her life as an artist."

The Amish follow a simple way of life, with no electricity, no cars and no modern conveniences.

Different Kinds of Amish

Most Amish fall into one of four orders:

- Swartzentruber—This is the strictest of the Amish groups. They avoid many things that the other groups will not, such as bicycles, Velcro, battery-operated lanterns, and buttons, rejecting them as too worldly.
- Andy Weaver—Slightly less conservative that the Swartzentruber group.
- Old Order—The most common Amish group. They will accept the use of technologies they will not own; for example, they will ride in cars driven by non-Amish people.
- New Order—This term refers to a number of groups that split away from the Old Order Amish in the 1960s. They live simply, much like the other Amish groups, but they allow electricity and telephones, as well as the use of motorized vehicles.

Even within these orders there can be a great deal of variety, in terms of individual beliefs and practices.

Opposite page: During a period called Rumspringa, Amish teenagers are given the chance to experience the world outside their community and to decide if they want to be baptized into the church. It is perhaps a surprise to outsiders that as many as 85% to 90% of teenagers choose to remain Amish and join the church.

The Amish life is full of *mystique* for those who know only what they have seen on movies, on television, or in books. In some parts of the United States, horse-drawn Amish buggies are a common sight, but few outsiders know what goes on inside an Amish community.

The Amish believe in a simple and plain life. They do not use electricity or modern technology, although many work with the "English"—the non-Amish—and are comfortable using technology through these contacts.

The Amish religion is central to their beliefs. They believe that they are to be separate from the rest of the world, living peaceably among their neighbors but not joining their neighbors' non-Amish practices. They also believe deeply in humility, that they should submit to the will of God in all things, putting God and their community above their individual wishes.

For Susie, this humility translates into being happy with her life. She likes being

Rumspringa

The term literally means "running around," and is used to refer to the period between about 16 and baptism into the Amish church as an adult. This is often a time when Amish young people explore their boundaries and how they feel about being Amish. Rumspringa has become known through the documentary *The Devil's Playground*, by Lucy Walker, and the book *Rumspringa: To Be or Not to Be Amish*, by Tom Shachtman, which show Amish teens drinking, having sex, and dealing drugs. People often believe that these Amish are typical, and that their parents and elders accept and condone such behavior, but the truth is that such rebellion is rare among the Amish.

Amish. She loves her family and her community. At one point, she began selling her paintings to a local gallery. They did well, and financially she was successful. Susie felt herself being pulled in by the success. She liked it, but that in itself bothered her.

One day, when her youngest son was about a year old, she told Louise, "I'm coming to understand that he and my other children are much more important than painting." She gave up painting for a time, focusing on her family.

"It was like a death," she said later. "I did not paint for six months. Until I finally came to terms with myself and came to understand that God doesn't mind if I do this."

She believes that, as a Christian, she may be an artist but she may not be a great artist. "Take van Gogh, for example," she said. "He just went away from his life. He forgot about everything and everyone and just painted. I can't do that."

Her desire to be content with her life is part of what drives Susie, and it is her deepest wish for her children's lives as well. "I am happy with what each of my children is right now," Susie said. "Why wait until they are grown to see what they will become? Each one of my children is a whole and complete person right now. Too many of us think if we just have one more thing, we will be happy. This I try to instill in my children—to be content with what they have. To be themselves right now."

Amish practices differ from community to community. While their religious beliefs are quite similar, along with their principles of humility and of separation from the world, they vary in how they interpret these principles.

What Do You Think?

What role does family play in Susie's life? How has her commitment to her family shaped her life? How does the religious community where she lives shape her beliefs about her family? Do you admire her beliefs and the decisions she has made because of them? Why or why not?

HEADLINES

(From "Amish Sect's Values Cause Conflict with Cambria County Building Codes" by Robin Acton, *Pittsburgh Tribune-Review*, 24 May 2009, http://www.pittsburghlive.com/x/pittsburghtrib/news/regional/s_626584.html)

When she wakes from restless sleep in the middle of the night, Susan Miller thinks about the man who put her family out of their rural Blacklick Township farm.

The Amish mother would like to talk to Cambria County Judge Norman Krumenacker, who ordered the house, barns and outbuildings padlocked because she and her husband John violated building codes and sewage regulations at their 49.5-acre homestead.

"I sat up in bed the other night, and I was thinking that I feel bad he has to do this to us. I wanted to write him a letter to tell him I'm praying for him," Miller said. "I don't feel anger. I actually pity him."

The Millers and other Amish in the *ultraconservative* Swartzentruber sect have reached an *impasse* in a clash of culture, religion and law with government agencies responsible for protecting public health and safety. Although two families were forced to leave their homes and one man has been jailed, the Amish say they aren't defending themselves because aggression, confrontation and violence—like the regulations they're refusing to follow—are against their religion.

The Amish want to use outhouses with homemade 250-gallon holding tanks to collect waste at two new homes and a school. They'd planned to treat the waste with lime and then spread it across their fields for fertilizer.

The law permits outhouses in new construction but stipulates either that tanks under 5,000 gallons be precast or the homeowners must provide engineers' specifications to show they are built properly. Homeowners must follow testing guidelines for treating the waste.

The Amish say the modern guidelines would force them to use technology.

"I don't think we can do what they want us to do, even if it means giving up our home," John Miller said. "I'd like to find a compromise, but we can't go against our religion."

Deborah Sedlmeyer, director of the Cambria County Sewage Enforcement Agency, said her agency cannot practice selective enforcement.

"They choose a simple life. That's OK, but they must do it legally," she said.

Compared with peers with lower levels of religiosity (in terms of importance assigned to religion and frequency of prayer), adolescents who were more religious exhibited higher levels of self-control and were less likely to use alcohol or marijuana, and less likely to abuse any chemical substance.

Religion is most important in the simplicity of the Amish culture. . . .

The Amish, who do not have an attorney, say they offered to pump their smaller tanks more frequently and treat the waste using "a recipe" developed by sewage officials.

"We're not trying to ruin other people's wells, but we can't use their testing equipment because it's against our religion," member Eli Zook said.

Last fall, Sedlmeyer's office and the Cambria County Building Code Enforcement Agency filed civil complaints against the Amish. In October and again in January, the judge ordered them to meet state and municipal regulations.

In March, Krumanecker shut down the school and ordered Andy Swartzentruber to serve 90 days in jail on a contempt of court charge for failing to bring its two outhouses up to standards. He is expected to be released June 14 from the Cambria County Prison. Jack Crislip, a planning supervisor with the state Department of Environmental Protection, said no one wanted to jail the Amish. He said the judge, county officials and DEP representatives visited one farm to try to help them.

He said his agency offered to compromise by permitting the Amish to use 1,000-gallon holding tanks if they obtained permits and provided information to prove the tanks are watertight, structurally sound and easily accessible for cleaning. However, he said there are other problems with indoor plumbing systems, which pump untreated wastewater from bathing, cleaning and laundry directly onto the surface of the ground.

"It was probably the most amicable meeting I've ever had with people who didn't agree with us," Crislip said. "We told them what needed to be done to comply and they just said, 'No.'"

Finally, the families ran out of chances.

On May 8, the judge ordered them to leave their homes until they comply with the law. Three days later, they packed their buggies with clothing, food and personal items and put cows and horses out to pasture as sheriff's deputies padlocked their houses.

Community reaction was mixed, with some neighbors pleased that the court refused to give them special treatment. But Northern Cambria Councilman Wilbur "Willie" Kelly, a friend of the Amish for the decade since he helped a sect member shoe a horse along the highway, said he's angered that they're being forced to go against their religious beliefs.

"In our culture, if people were being wrenched out of their homes, you'd see anger and fist-fighting and the police would be called," Kelly said. "With these people, it's nothing but silence. They just want to live their lives peacefully."

Sheriff's deputies Jake Kehn and Clint Divido pad-locked the empty barns May 15. Watching them from beneath the brim of his straw hat, Andy Miller, 5, scuffed clumps of mud with the duct-taped tips of his battered boots as he moved back and forth in a red Roadmaster wagon.

"We're just following court orders," Kehn told the boy's parents. "Good luck."

John Miller, shaking his head at his partially finished two-story home, said he does not know what to do next.

He and his wife and son sleep in a single room at his parents' farmhouse. They have their own table for meals, eaten on borrowed dishes, in the wash house where his mother and sisters do the family's laundry.

"We still have a lot; it's just different," his wife said, reassuring him. "We can get by with a lot less now."

What Do You Think?

Did the town of Northern Cambria do the right thing by enforcing their laws with the Amish? Why or why not? Imagine what it would be like for you if you were a young person in this Amish community. In what ways is this community's religion affecting the lives of all its families?

HEADLINES

(From "Westward Ho! Amish Escaping Crowds, Prices in East" by Alysia Patterson, *Seattle Times*, 6 June 2009, http://seattletimes. nwsource.com/html/nationworld/2009308583_apusamishheadwest. html)

A new road sign cautions drivers to watch for Amish horse-drawn carriages in the valley beneath Colorado's Sangre de Cristo Mountains. Highway pull-offs and dedicated horse-and-buggy paths are in the works.

Amid the serenity and isolation of southern Colorado, hamlets like Westcliffe, La Jara and Monte Vista are welcoming Amish families who are moving West to escape high land prices and community overcrowding back East in Indiana, Ohio and Pennsylvania.

"The reason we moved out West is the farm land is a little bit cheaper and it's not as heavily populated, a little more open space and a little more opportunity for young people to get started with their own farms," said Ben Coblentz, a 47-year-old alfalfa farmer from Indiana. "The general public seems to have a little slower pace of life than what it was back east. Everybody here respects us."

Of an estimated 231,000 Amish nationwide, more than 60 percent still live in Ohio, Pennsylvania and Indiana.

But from 2002 to 2008, Colorado's Amish population went from zero to more than 400, according to the Young Center for Anabaptist and Pietist Studies at Pennsylvania's Elizabethtown College. Montana, with an estimated 540 Amish, and Colorado now have the westernmost Amish settlements in the U.S. Colorado ranks seventh in the nation in Amish immigration, according to the Young Center.

Coblentz moved to Monte Vista four years ago with his wife, Laura, and their four children. They were the 12th Amish family to settle in the area.

"There are 28 families now," Coblentz said. "Two more families are moving in next week."

Others will likely follow.

"I see it happening where there will be a lot more Amish making a westward movement, just because of the land prices," said Stephen Scott, a research associate at the Young Center.

Cropland is worth an average $1,400 per acre in Colorado, compared with $6,000 in Pennsylvania and about $4,000 in Ohio and Indiana, according to a 2007 census by the U.S. Department of Agriculture. Cropland values in Pennsylvania jumped 17 percent from 2006 to 2007 but by only 6 percent in Colorado.

The Amish are a Christian denomination who trace their roots to the Protestant Reformation in 16th-century Europe and migrated to North America in the 18th and 19th centuries. Over the last century, many have turned to nonfarm work such as family owned shops. They avoid hooking up to the electrical grid because of a belief that doing so will lead to a dependence on the outside world.

Some eastern Amish families simply have outgrown their communities. The average Amish couple have seven children, and the total population doubles about every 20 years, said Dr. Thomas Meyers, a sociology professor at Goshen College in Indiana.

"There's an increasing need for land for young couples that want to get established," said Meyers.

Jim Austin, a commissioner in Colorado's Custer County, which includes Westcliffe, couldn't be happier about the newcomers.

"Our goal is hopefully to preserve this valley," Austin said about his efforts to bar development from the green meadows he calls home between the Sangre de Cristo and Wet mountains. "They are hardworking, down-to-earth, pretty simple folks. From what I see, I like it. They are going to be good neighbors."

An Amish family recently opened Yoder's Mountain View Furniture on Westcliffe's Main Street. On one recent day, a woman wearing a black apron, bonnet and long sleeves sat outside reading in one of the hand-crafted chairs advertised for sale. Business is slow, but Austin, his Amish neighbors and longstanding residents like it that way.

"I help them out and drive them to town whenever they need a ride," said Bruce Hornig, a Monte Vista farmer and Coblentz's neighbor. "Everybody out here in Colorado waves to everybody. The people are so much nicer."

Coblentz, like all Amish, dresses in plain clothes—black pants and a white or blue shirt. Women wear dresses, bonnets and aprons. He doesn't drive a car, use a computer, watch TV or allow a phone in the house, which he built from scratch. His family attends church every Sunday at a neighbor's house. His two school-age sons go to a community-run Amish school. His older son and daughter both married and moved to nearby farms.

"The reason we live the way we do is it seems to kind of separate us from the mainstream world, makes it a little easier to resist temptations—a quiet life," Coblentz said. "It doesn't make us any better. We're still human like everybody else. ... It makes it a little easier."

What Do You Think?

How does the author of this article feel about the Amish? (Respect? Confusion? Admiration? Contempt?) Coblentz, the Amish man interviewed in this article, says that the Amish way of life makes things "a little easier" for Amish families. What do you think he means? Imagine how you would feel if you were growing up in an Amish family. Would you want to leave behind your religion once you grew up—or would you be grateful to take an adult role in your community?

Chapter 4: Growing Up in a Conservative Christian Group

Terms to Understand

extricated: released from entanglement; got away from.

doctrine: a body of principles believed and taught by a group.

testimony: public profession of faith.

congregation: a group of people who meet together for religious worship.

traumatic: psychologically painful.

insulated: separated, protected from outside influences.

taboo: forbidden or unacceptable in a society.

deviations: instances of turning away from the standard or norm.

divergence: moving away from.

transition: change, movement from one position, state, or condition to another.

empirical: proven by or guided by experience or experiment.

There's a two-inch scar on the back of Jaime Seba's right ankle that she once attributed to a smiting from her Heavenly Father. At age seventeen, she was leaving the house to venture into a movie theatre for the first time when her shoe caught on the metal screen door, causing the gash. Although she had already *extricated* herself from her church, a strict Christian sect that forbade numerous mainstream cultural activities including movie-going, the injury was clearly punishment from God.

"The funniest thing is that I was going to see *Mr. Holland's Opus*, which is such a benign and wholesome film," she says now, thirteen years later. "And when it came out on video, I would have been able to rent it. But seeing it in a theatre was sinful. It made no sense."

Baptized into the religion only a few days after her birth in 1979, Jaime grew up surrounded by its *doctrine*. Her mother Valerie had converted from Catholicism after meeting her future husband Joe, who had adopted the religion with his family as a child. Working tirelessly for the church, Valerie and Joe immediately included Jaime and her brother Jason, older by twenty-two months, in their campaign to "bring *testimony*" to others. Venturing out of their white suburban comfort zone to foster a relationship with their new religious community, the small family clapped and sang gospel music with the mostly African-American *congregation* that attended their church.

But their religion didn't make the family immune to the realities of life. By Jaime's fourth birthday, Valerie and Joe were separated, and eventually they divorced. As a single mother, Valerie worked full time and went to school in the evening, something she was only able to do because of the kindness of a fellow churchgoer who provided free babysitting services. Despite relying on public assistance to make ends meet, Valerie always managed to drop 10 percent of her money into the collection box at church.

> **Terms to Understand**
>
> **ecumenical:** universal; especially relating to the whole Christian church.
> **sociological:** dealing with the issues having to do with relations between people and groups of people.
> **intergenerational:** involving people from more than one generation or age group.
> **vested:** having been given authority or rights.
> **secular:** relating to things that are not religious or spiritual.

"Divorce is usually such a *traumatic* thing, but we were just so *insulated* by the church," Jaime says. "The church was always the focus, so much that it didn't seem like that big of a deal when my dad left."

There are many branches of Christianity. This diagram shows the multitude of denominations just within the Protestant movement.

Life continued according to the church's plan. Every weekend Jaime and Jason attended Sunday school classes, followed by two sermons. Monday evenings held more religious education, followed by an evening cleaning the church on Tuesday. Another sermon was given on Wednesdays, and Thursdays were designated evenings when priests would visit the homes of parishioners. Fri-

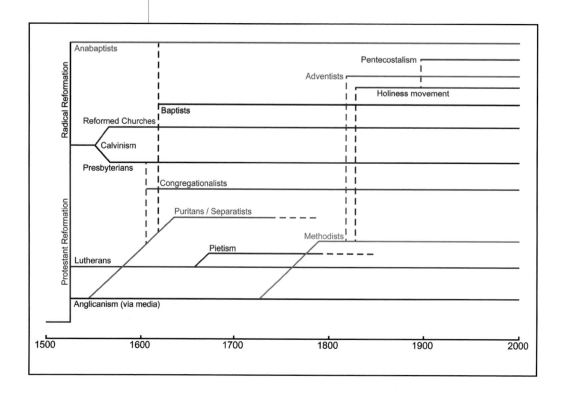

day evenings were for socializing with other families in the church. Saturdays were spent preparing for the Sabbath, including turning off the television by 7 p.m.

"The structure was good for us as kids," Jaime says. "It kept us out of trouble. Mom always knew where we were and what we were doing. But it was definitely limiting."

In addition to staying out of movie theatres, the community did not celebrate Halloween. Thanksgiving was observed in October. Christmas was a major holiday, but it was devoid of trees or many of the other commonly recognized symbols of the season. Dancing was not permitted. Most elements of pop culture—MTV, posters of rock stars, professional sports, concerts—were off limits. Even bowling alleys were prohibited. Men wore cropped haircuts and no jewelry. Women earnestly worked toward their destiny of being wives and mothers, with college and a career a mere afterthought.

Needless to say, these restrictions often set the children apart from their classmates. But even that was made simpler by the constant presence of other church members. People from outside the church, known as "The World," were rarely part of the social circle.

But for all her strict adherence to the tenets of the church, Valerie's maternal instincts led her to instill her strong personal values in her children. When the children were still small, their babysitter and a close family friend from the church came out as gay. The

Tithing—giving 10 percent of your income to God—is a religious practice followed by many Christians.

issue was so *taboo* within their church that it was rarely even discussed. But Valerie made her feelings perfectly clear.

"You know Richie, and you love Richie," she told her children. "No matter what you hear people say, remember that he's still the Richie you love. And there's nothing wrong with him."

Such *deviations* from the Path of Faith, though hugely influential on her family, were minor blips in the grand scheme of their religious life. But when Valerie remarried and the family relocated, they were forced to confront the harsh reality of hypocrisy.

Though they attended a congregation of the same religion, it was worlds away from the principles that had dictated their lives for more than fifteen years. The priest wore a gold chain around his neck. The children went to movies and dances. And the daily activities were whittled down to services twice a week. For Valerie, the collapse of the beliefs that had guided her parenting and personal identity led to a crisis of faith and a parting from the church. Jason went away to college and his own personal voyage of exploration. Jaime stayed the longest, participating in the church youth group.

Jaime's *divergence* from the Path came during a youth group meeting when someone asked the church's view on homosexuality. The answer: "It's a sin. We love the sinner, but we hate the sin." A friend in the room whom Jaime suspected was gay was clearly upset.

> Researchers have found that individuals who were raised by parents who attended church are less apt to report that they feel lonely, depressed, or lacking in self-worth as adults.

Not all Christian churches preach that homosexuality is a sin. Many, like this Boston-area church, welcome everyone and advertise the fact with rainbow flags and statements of inclusion.

"When I saw the look on his face, it broke my heart," she says. "And I couldn't wrap my head around it. Dancing was a sin. Bowling was a sin. Gay was a sin. It seemed so silly. It didn't make sense. And for the first time, I actually saw how it impacted my life."

Before long, Jaime had also moved away from the church. Years later, as she reflects on her upbringing and the impact it had on her family and her personal development, she has a new perspective. And she sees her scar a bit differently.

"I don't regret any of it," she says. "I learned the value of my mind and thinking for myself. I used to think God was punishing me. But now I see it as part of my growth, that *transition* from being told who you are to discovering who you are. It may be painful, but it's just a part of life. And it stays with you forever."

> Researchers have found that children are less likely to have behavior problems at school if either of their parents (particularly their mothers) attend religious services than children whose parents did not attend religious services at all.

What Do You Think?

Jaime left her church when she grew older, yet in some ways she seems grateful for its influence? Why do you think that is? In what ways do you think the church was good for her and her family? When the church played such a positive role in the family's life for so many years, why do you think all three family members eventually decided to leave it behind?

HEADLINES

(From "Why Are Kids Leaving the Church? The Answer Lies in Parents" by Dudley Chancey, *The Christian Chronicle*, June 2009, http://www.christianchronicle.org/article2158796~Why_are_kids_leaving_the_church%3F_The_answer_lies_in_parents)

I have yet to find the definitive, *empirical* study as to why kids leave church, although it is a very hot topic right now across the *ecumenical* world. But here is what we do know—kids are leaving! This is not news.

Many of our kids leave high school, go off to college and take a break from church. The bad news—the Barna Group and other researchers point out that, for the first time in their ongoing studies of church life, many of these kids are not returning to the church when they marry and have kids.

Why is this happening? What can we do about it?

Only God and parents really know how delicate children are. While many teens "commit" their life to Christ, not much happens before or after that for many of our "churched" teens. In *sociological* studies, a majority of moms and dads report that religion and faith are among the most important influences in their lives. And yet, over and over again, this is not lived out. The church—and particularly youth workers—get the blame for teens not being spiritual enough to make it on the outside. In "Why Christian Kids Rebel: Trading

Heartache for Hope," Tim Kimmel writes that some kids see their parents treating faith like a hobby, so they follow suit. We know that children's perceptions of their parents' religious beliefs—and the accuracy of these perceptions — influence the acceptance of these beliefs. . . .

Over and over in sociological research, parents (typically mom first and dad second) are the primary influence in teens' lives. Youth ministers, preachers, church and youth groups are down the list, though they do have some influence.

How can parents fulfill their roles? It actually isn't that difficult, it just takes time. In "Raising the Bar: Ministry to Youth in the New Millennium," Alvin Reid reminds us that only 34 percent of North American families eat one meal together each day. The average father spends eight minutes per day with his children. (That includes meals and watching TV.) Only 12 percent of families pray together. The average couple spends only four minutes of uninterrupted time together a day.

We do not have time for relationships. That's what our behavior says to our children. Perhaps we are too busy, or we do not feel adequate to be the spiritual leader of our children or our faith is not real for us.

The oft-quoted Shema from Deuteronomy is about spending time with our families and "doing ministry" with our families. Youth and children's ministries can assist parents in their roles, but they can't replace those roles. We sometimes build $4 million buildings for our children, only to watch them walk away from those buildings after graduation.

While thinking about "family ministry" is not new, it is still not the norm in North American churches.

Churches are basically doing the same thing parents are doing—"dropping off the kids" with youth ministries. We have put the concept of *intergenerational* ministry on the shelf. Sometimes we aren't even doing "big" church together. We have separate assemblies for our youths.

Is it any wonder that our children have nothing *vested* in church when they walk out as high school seniors?

Children's church and youth group meetings are over. Some of our campus ministries attempt to keep that experience going, but it is a very poor attempt, if one checks out the percentages of our children at these universities and then counts on a Wednesday night how many attend the college-age Bible class.

In the book *Family-Based Youth Ministry*, Mark Devries reminds churches that "there is no such thing as successful youth ministry that isolates teenagers from the community of faith." I am not advocating that we toss children and youth ministries from the church. I would strongly suggest that they be used as tools to equip parents to disciple their own children.

Children will look as much like Jesus as their parents and fellow church members do. Kids will follow Jesus through college—and for the rest of their lives—if they have parents that do likewise, and if that they can see older Christians modeling that behavior. Even some *secular* researchers stress the importance of having a "community of shepherds" around our children. Shouldn't this be the church?

We know that children rely on their parents and other adults around them for support and affirmation, but we don't make time to sit with our children and tell them about the faith that sustains us. . . .

Parents, bottom line, it is still your job to rear your children and teach them to have faith in God. Elders, it is your job to shepherd our souls. Please stop sending money to Africa, Brazil, Honduras and other foreign countries to save souls when our own children are walking out on God. Please rethink church and ministry as equipping people to become mature in Christ. . . .

Moms and dads at home, and elders and ministers at our churches, wake up! Let's repent. Let's recommit.

Let's walk and talk and do our faith with our children.

We have to disciple our own children and teach them to make disciples. It is a continuing process. We must not skip—or lose—a generation!

What Do You Think?

Describe the worldview held by the author of this article? In what ways do you agree with what he says? In what ways do you disagree? Do you think that what he says applies only to his own religious community (conservative, evangelical Christians) or do you think it applies to other religious communities as well? Do you know how other religious communities—for instance, Jewish, Muslim, or Hindu families—pass on their faith to the next generation? How do their practices differ from Christians'?

Find Out More

BOOKS

Bass, Dorothy C. and Don. C. Richter. *Way to Live: Christian Practices for Teens.* Nashville, Tenn.: Upper Room Books, 2002.

Bayoumi, Moustafa. *How Does It Feel to Be a Problem?: Being Young and Arab in America.* New York: Penguin, 2008.

Edgell, Penny. *Religion and Family in a Changing Society.* Princeton, N.J.: Princeton University Press, 2006.

Gaskins, Pearl Fuyo. *I Believe In . . . Christian, Jewish, and Muslim Young People Speak About Their Faith.* Peru, Ill.: Carus Publishing Company, 2004.

Gay, Kathlyn. *Religion and Spirituality in America: The Ultimate Teen Guide.* Lanham, Md.: Scarecrow Press, 2006.

Hafiz, Dilara, Imran Hafiz, and Yasmine Hafiz. *The American Muslim Teenager's Handbook.* Phoenix, Ariz.: Acacia Publishing, 2007.

Hunter, David. *Teen Life Among the Amish and Other Alternative Communities: Choosing a Lifestyle.* Broomall, Penn.: Mason Crest, 2007.

Singer, Rabbi Arne. *The Outsider's Guide to Orthodox Judaism.* Mountainside, N.J., 2008.

Stevick, Pauline. *Beyond the Plain and Simple: A Patchwork of Amish Lives.* Kent, Ohio: Kent State University Press, 2007.

Williams, Mary E. *Religion in America.* Farmington Hills, Mich.: Greenhaven Press, 2005.

ON THE INTERNET

The Amish and the Plain People of Lancaster County, PA
www.800padutch.com/amish.shtml

Christianity.com
www.christianity.com

Interfaith
www.interfaith.org

Interfaith Youth Core
www.ifyc.org

Muslims in America
www.muslimsinamerica.org

Religious Tolerance
www.religioustolerance.org

Bibliography

Chopich, Erika J. "Do Children Need Religion?" *Beliefnet*. www.
beliefnet.com/Love-Family/Parenting/2004/02/Do-Children-
Need-Religion.aspx. Accessed 6-10-2009.

Patel, Eboo. *Acts of Faith: The Story of an American Muslim,
the Struggle for the Soul of a Generation.* Boston: Beacon Press,
2007.

Patel, Eboo. "We Are Each Other's Business." N*PR: This I Believe*. 7 Nov. 2005. http://www.npr.org/templates/story/story.
php?storyId=4989625.

Stoltzfus, Louise. *Amish Women: Lives and Stories.* Intercourse,
Penn.: Good Books, 1994.

Index

adopt 6, 49
abuse 13, 14, 39

belief
   individual 11, 34
   religious 24, 37, 41, 46, 52, 53
buggies 35, 41

Catholic 23, 24, 49
Christian 11, 13, 27, 37, 49, 51, 55, 58, 59
compromise 39, 40
conservative 20, 30, 32, 34, 38, 48, 59
court 14, 4042
culture 20, 25, 26, 28, 30, 32, 34, 35, 45, 51

death 12, 19, 37
divorce 49, 50

faith 77, 8, 14, 15, 18, 19, 22, 48, 52, 55, 56, 58, 59

Gallup Poll 6, 7, 13

hate 23, 53
homosexual 6, 53

immigration 44
Islam 16–19, 27, 29, 31

Jewish 20, 24, 27, 59
justice 14, 17, 23

leader 12, 13, 21, 54
legal 6, 39
love 23, 32, 56,

marriage 13

public school 28
psychology 11, 28, 48

ritual 16, 17, 22

spiritual 8, 11, 49, 56

terrorism 21, 26, 30
tradition 8, 10–12, 14, 20, 24, 29

university 27, 29, 57

About the Author and the Consultant

AUTHOR

Sheila Stewart has written several dozen educational books for young people. She lives with her children in Western New York and works as a writer and editor.

CONSULTANT

Gallup has studied human nature and behavior for more than seventy years. Gallup's reputation for delivering relevant, timely, and visionary research on what people around the world think and feel is the cornerstone of the organization. Gallup employs many of the world's leading scientists in management, economics, psychology, and sociology, and its consultants assist leaders in identifying and monitoring behavioral economic indicators worldwide. Gallup consultants help organizations boost organic growth by increasing customer engagement and maximizing employee productivity through measurement tools, coursework, and strategic advisory services. Gallup's 2,000 professionals deliver services at client organizations, through the Web, at Gallup University's campuses, and in forty offices around the world.